Diamonds
and
Gemstones

Ron Edwards and Lisa Dickie

 Crabtree Publishing Company
www.crabtreebooks.com

Crabtree Publishing Company

www.crabtreebooks.com

PMB 16A, 350 Fifth Avenue,
Suite 3308,
New York, NY 10118

612 Welland Avenue,
St. Catharines,
Ontario, Canada
L2M 5V6

73 Lime Walk,
Headington,
Oxford, 0X3 7AD
United Kingdom

Coordinating editor: Ellen Rodger

Project editor: Sean Charlebois

Editor: Carrie Gleason

Contributing author: Rona Arato

Production coordinator and designer: Rosie Gowsell

Design: Brad Colotelo, Rosie Gowsell

Indexer: Wendy Scavuzzo

Production assistant: Samara Parent

Scanning technician: Arlene Arch-Wilson

Art director: Rob MacGregor

Photo research: Allison Napier

Prepress and printing: Worzalla Publishing Company

Photographs: D. AUBERT/CORBIS SYGMA/MAGMA: p. 18 (top); BILL BACHMAN: p. 14, p. 27; Bettmann/CORBIS/ MAGMA: p. 19 (bottom); Jonathan Blair/CORBIS/MAGMA: p. 25 (top); CP SOURCE/Adrian Wyld: p. 19 (top); CP/Source Jacques Boissinot: p. 28; CP Source/MARTIAL TREZZINI: cover, p. 7 (bottom); Daly & Newton/Getty Images: p. 7 (top); George B. Diebold/ CORBIS/MAGMA: p. 1; VO TRUNG DUNG/CORBIS SYGMA/ MAGMA: p. 26; Jack Fields/CORBIS/MAGMA: p. 16; V. Fleming/Photo Researchers, Inc.: p. 21 (top); Owen Franken/ CORBIS /MAGMA: p. 22; Lowell Georgia/CORBIS/MAGMA: p. 24; Edward Kimsman/Photo Researchers, Inc.: page headers; LAWRENCE LAWRY/SCIENCE PHOTO LIBRARY: p. 29; Charles O'Rear/CORBIS/MAGMA: p. 17 (top), p. 21 (top), p. 22 (bottom); photodisc/Getty Images: p. 8 (top); H. David Seawell/CORBIS/ MAGMA: p. 25 (bottom); Marc Schlossman: p. 6; Thinkstock LLC: p. 15; Luis Veiga: p. 29; Teun Voeten: p. 23; Larry Williams/ CORBIS/MAGMA: p. 9 (top); Adam Woolfitt/CORBIS/MAGMA: p. 21 (bottom); Dr. Paul A. Zahl/Photo Researchers, Inc.: p. 9 (bottom)

Illustrations: Dan Pressman: p. 10, p. 11, p. 12, p. 13, p. 18, p. 20, p. 21; Margaret Amy Reiach: contents

Map: Jim Chernishenko: p. 17

Cover: A flawless, or perfect, diamond is one of nature's rarest and most beautiful creations. A book written in the 700s in India claims that the flash of a flawless diamond can conquer enemies, ensure health, happiness, and prosperity, and protect against danger.

Title page: For thousands of years, diamonds and gems have been cut and polished for jewelry.

Contents: Digging for diamonds in an open-pit mine in Africa.

Back cover: The Imperial State Crown of England contains 2,783 diamonds, 277 pearls, seventeen sapphires, eleven emeralds, and five rubies.

Published by
Crabtree Publishing Company

Cataloging-in-Publication Data

Edwards, Ron, 1947-
 Diamonds and gemstones / Ron Edwards & Lisa Dickie.
  p. cm. -- (Rocks, minerals, and resources)
 Includes index.
 ISBN 0-7787-1414-4 (rlb) -- ISBN 0-7787-1446-2 (pb)
 1. Diamonds--Juvenile literature. 2. Precious stones--Juvenile literature. I. Dickie, Lisa. II. Title. III. Series.
TN990.E39 2004
553.8'2--dc22

                                        2004000810
                                        LC

Contents

Curse of the Hope Diamond

The dazzling blue Hope Diamond has a blood-soaked history. It was stolen from an idol of an Indian goddess by French merchant Jean Tavernier, who sold it to King Louis XIV of France. Tavernier was later killed by wild dogs in Russia, and the king's son and his wife, Marie Antoinette, were beheaded during the French Revolution. In the years that followed, the diamond was blamed for financial ruin, death, and insanity. Many people still believe the Hope Diamond is cursed.

The Story of Diamonds and Gemstones

Throughout history, kings and queens, nobles and commoners have been awed, tempted, and inspired by the beauty of diamonds and gemstones. Diamonds were believed to conquer enemies, ensure health, happiness, and prosperity, and protect against danger. In the 1600s and 1700s, French and Italian kings believed diamonds and gemstones had **supernatural** powers and wore them as protection in battle.

Sparkling Stones

Gemstones are rare and beautiful minerals **found in the Earth that are cut and polished for jewelry. Some gemstones, such as diamonds, rubies, sapphires, and emeralds are called precious stones because they are beautiful, rare, and durable, which means they cannot be scratched. Other gemstones are called semi-precious.**

Diamonds

Diamonds are the hardest natural substance on Earth, and this hardness means they last longer than other gemstones. Diamonds were discovered in India where they were called *vajra,* meaning "thunderbolt."

Stones of many colors

Diamonds are sometimes called "ice" because a typical diamond is clear and cold to the touch. Colorless diamonds are made of pure **carbon** and are the most valuable. When other **chemicals** mix with the carbon, the diamonds turn different colors, including brown, violet, pink, and black. Red is the rarest color for diamonds. Brightly colored diamonds are called "fancies."

The most valuable diamonds are colorless. Light passing through diamonds disperses, or spreads out, like a rainbow through a prism.

Diamonds in history

Throughout history, kings, queens, and wealthy people owned the largest most beautiful stones. Some, such as the Koh-I-Nor and Orloff diamonds, have become very famous.

Koh-I-Nor

The original Koh-I-Nor diamond weighed 186 **karats**. It came from India and its name means "Mountain of Light." The stone was cut down in size during the reign of Queen Victoria (1837-1901) and is now part of England's Crown Jewels.

The Orloff

The Orloff diamond, now in the Diamond Treasury in Moscow, Russia, originally weighed 300 karats. It was stolen by a French soldier from the eye of a statue of a god, in the temple of Sri Rangen, India.

(above) Diamonds have been associated with wealth and extravagance, shown here with this dog's expensive collar.

(left) The word diamond comes from the Greek word adamao, meaning "I tame" or "I subdue." The adjective adamas was used to describe the hardest substance known, and eventually came to mean diamond.

Rubies and sapphires

After diamonds, rubies and sapphires are the hardest and most valued gems. The word ruby comes from the **Latin** word *rubrum* for red, and sapphire, from *sapphires*, from the ancient Greek word for blue. Rubies and sapphires are made from a colorless mineral called corundum. When the minerals iron and titanium are present in the stone, the corundum becomes a blue sapphire. A small amount of the mineral chromium turns corundum into a red ruby.

Rubies and sapphires come from the mineral corundum.

Emeralds are the fourth hardest gemstone.

Emeralds

The word emerald comes from the Greek word "smaragdus," meaning "green." Emeralds were first mined in Egypt 4,000 years ago. In the 1700s, the Spanish discovered emeralds while searching for gold in Mexico and Peru. The best emeralds still come from South America. A form of the mineral beryl, emeralds are treasured for their rarity and beautiful green color.

Organic gemstones

Not all gemstones are minerals. Some gemstones begin as, or are formed by, living **organisms**. These types of gemstones are called organic gemstones, and they are not as durable as mineral gemstones.

Most pearls today are cultured, which means people insert a tiny bit of shell into an oyster so that it will create a pearl.

Types of organic gems

The four kinds of organic gems are coral, pearl, amber, and jet. Coral is found in the oceans. It is made from the skeletons of tiny animals that once lived underwater. Pearls are made by underwater mollusks, or shellfish. When a tiny piece of food or shell gets into the mollusk's shell, the mollusk coats it with a protective substance called nacre, or mother-of-pearl. Amber is the resin, or sap, of ancient pine trees. Over millions of years, the resin was buried and **fossilized**, and turned into amber. Jet is a black gem made from fossilized wood and other plant life.

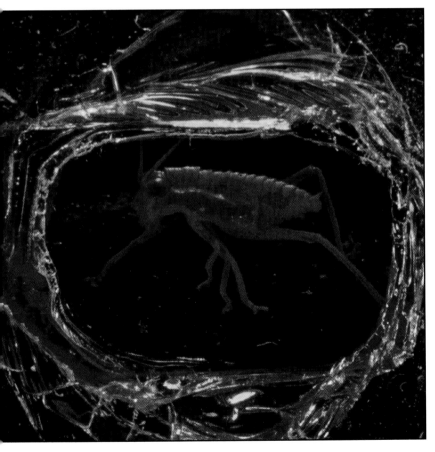

A grasshopper trapped in amber 40 million years ago.

Mineral Gemstones

Most gemstones were formed deep inside the Earth billions of years ago. Heat and pressure within the Earth turned minerals into gemstones. Today, gemstones are found in rocks.

Minerals and crystals

Rocks are made up of different minerals. Minerals are natural, non-living substances. The hardness, color, weight, and the way it breaks is different for every mineral. Most mineral gemstones are crystals. Crystals have **atoms** that are arranged in a regular, three-dimensional repeating pattern. The biggest and best gemstone crystals form in small cracks of rock, called veins. Veins form when hot water or **magma** containing minerals rises up through the Earth. When the water or magma cools, the crystals form.

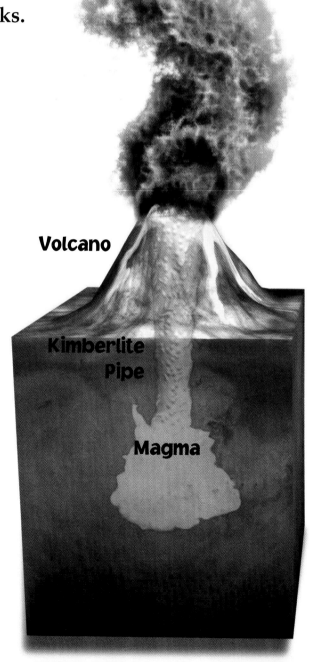

Volcano

Kimberlite Pipe

Magma

Diamonds are carried to the surface of the Earth by magma. Magma travels upward through shafts called pipes.

Gems in the rock cycle

The solid part of the Earth's surface, or crust, is made up of rocks. Rocks are formed over millions of years in a process called the rock cycle. This process occurs when magma, from deep within the Earth, erupts from volcanoes. When magma erupts it is called lava. When lava cools it forms a type of rock called igneous rock. Diamonds are found in igneous rock.

Over many years, rock is worn down into pieces by the weather. Rivers carry the bits of rock to the ocean, where they pile up on the bottom and create new rocks. As many layers build up, a type of rock called sedimentary rock forms. Opal and turquoise are gems formed when mineral-rich water seeps into the rock. Sedimentary rock sinks back into the Earth where it melts into magma. The process repeats as magma erupts again.

Rocks that change

Metamorphic rocks change into different kinds of rock by extreme pressure and heat under the Earth's crust. The heat and pressure causes new minerals to form in the rock. Gemstones such as jade, garnet, and some rubies and sapphires are found in metamorphic rock.

Diamond deposits

Eroded cone

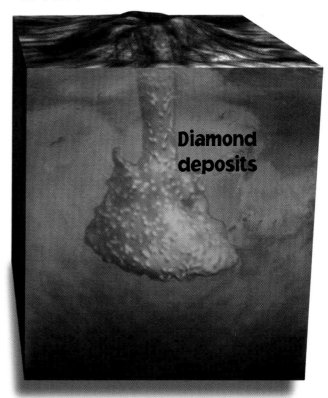

Diamond deposits

Where are the diamonds?

There are two main types of diamond deposits: primary and secondary. Primary deposits are diamonds found in pipes, or columns of rock extending from under Earth's crust where the diamonds form, to the surface. Secondary deposits are found further away from where the diamonds formed. Millions of years ago when a volcano erupted, it brought magma to the Earth's surface as lava. The lava contained crystals that became embedded in rock as the lava hardened. Over time, the rocks wore down and were carried into rivers and oceans. The first diamonds discovered were found in riverbeds, which are secondary deposits.

11

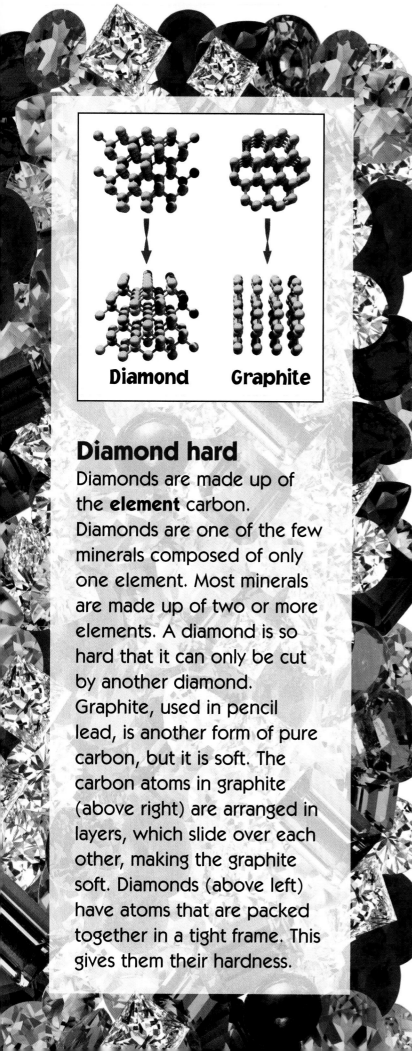

Diamond   **Graphite**

Diamond hard

Diamonds are made up of the **element** carbon. Diamonds are one of the few minerals composed of only one element. Most minerals are made up of two or more elements. A diamond is so hard that it can only be cut by another diamond. Graphite, used in pencil lead, is another form of pure carbon, but it is soft. The carbon atoms in graphite (above right) are arranged in layers, which slide over each other, making the graphite soft. Diamonds (above left) have atoms that are packed together in a tight frame. This gives them their hardness.

How diamonds form

Diamonds can be found in different types of deposits, but they all formed in the same way. Geologists, or scientists who study the Earth, believe that diamonds formed more than a billion years ago in the Earth's **mantle**, over 93 miles (150 kilometers) below the surface. In the mantle, magma containing the element carbon was heated to over 2,192° Fahrenheit (1,200° Celsius). This intense heat and pressure caused the carbon to form into crystals. When magma moved upward to the Earth's surface, it carried the carbon crystals, or diamonds, with it. As the magma hardened to form igneous rock, the diamonds became stuck in the rock and were also carried to the surface.

Kimberlite

Kimberlite is a kind of igneous rock. When kimberlite forms from magma in Earth's mantle, carbon crystals become embedded in this blue rock. Magma containing kimberlite was blasted up through the Earth's crust millions of years ago during volcanic eruptions.

Kimberlite pipes

Kimberlite acts as an "elevator," which brings diamonds, along with other crystals and rocks, to the Earth's surface. Today, columns of kimberlite containing diamonds, called kimberlite pipes, are buried underground. Geologists believe that kimberlite pipes are between 50 million and 1,600 million years old, while diamonds are between one billion and 3.3 billion years old. Kimberlite pipes are named after Kimberley, a town in South Africa that has a rich diamond deposit.

A kimberlite pipe

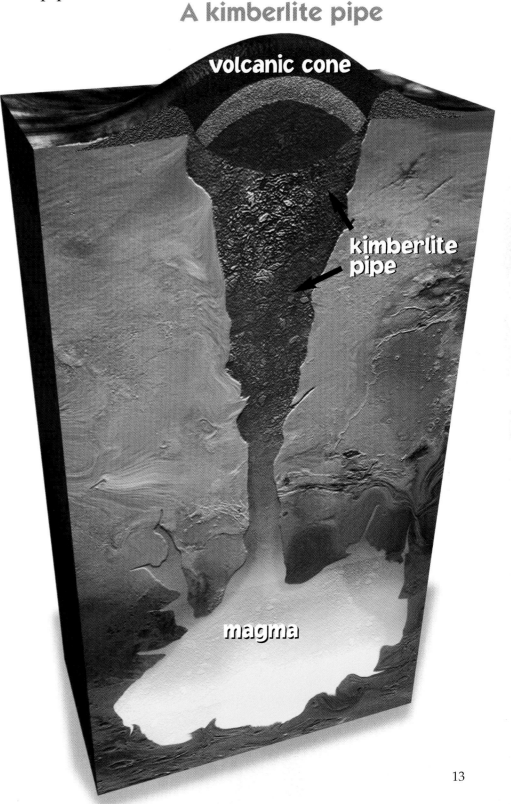

volcanic cone

kimberlite pipe

magma

Lamproite pipes

Another form of "elevator" that brings diamonds to the surface is a lamproite pipe. Lamproite is also an igneous rock. Lamproite pipes form when a violent volcanic eruption blasts a crater, or hole, in the Earth's surface. The lamproite lava fills the crater, forming a v-shaped deposit that can contain diamonds.

Diamonds are the most popular and well-known gemstone. For thousands of years they have represented wealth and power. Diamonds were found in riverbeds in India around 800 B.C. and India remained the main source of diamonds until supplies dwindled in the mid-1700s. Diamond hunters then began looking for new sources of the precious stone in South America and Africa.

Diamond rush

In 1867, a child playing near the Orange River that runs through the middle of South Africa found a "pretty pebble." He gave it to his neighbor, who identified it as a 21.25-karat brownish-yellow diamond. Two years later, a shepherd boy found an 85.50-karat diamond, later named the Star of Africa. The Star of Africa's discovery sent thousands of diamond **prospectors** rushing to where the giant stone was discovered. Several discoveries were made, including one on a farm owned by the De Beer brothers. At first, it was not difficult to mine the diamonds because they were close to the surface. As they became more difficult to reach, miners dug deep into the Earth.

An open-pit diamond mine in South Africa, owned by De Beer's, the world's largest diamond company.

Staking a claim

In 1871, British businessman Cecil Rhodes staked his first claim in the newly opened Kimberley diamond fields. Soon, Rhodes had many claims and in 1880, he formed the De Beers Mining Company, named after the De Beers family, on whose farm the most important find was made.

De Beers

Rhodes wanted to control the whole diamond industry in South Africa. In 1889, he pressured Lobengula, the king of Matabeleland, now in Zimbabwe, into selling him all of his people's mineral rights for a small amount of money. Working with the British South Africa Company, Rhodes developed his claims. In 1888, Rhodes merged his business. The new company, De Beers Consolidated Mines established a **monopoly** over the South African diamond industry. Today, De Beer's is a huge international company that controls most of the world's diamond production.

A girl's best friend?

In 1477, Archduke Maximillian of Austria presented his future bride, Mary of Burgundy, with a diamond ring. Mary wore the ring as a sign that she and the Duke would marry, but it took almost 500 years for diamond rings to become a popular engagement symbol. In 1948, the De Beer's diamond company launched the "A Diamond is Forever" advertising campaign. This was right after World War II, and soldiers were coming home and getting married. People wanted to feel good and diamonds became a symbol of their new lives. Soon, millions of people were buying diamonds when they became engaged. The increased demand for diamonds increased their value, as De Beers determined how many diamonds were for sale on the market.

Mining Gemstones

Prospectors are people who search for minerals. Diamond prospectors must know a great deal about the Earth before they can find diamonds. Prospectors and geologists look for diamonds in alluvial **deposits, in kimberlite pipes, and on ocean floors.**

Alluvial mining

Sand and dirt that have been moved from one place to another by flowing water, such as rivers and streams, are called alluvial deposits. This moving water also transports diamonds with the sand and dirt. To find alluvial deposits, prospectors look for a sunken area in riverbeds or dried up riverbeds, where water may have deposited diamonds. To get the diamonds, the top layer of rock in the riverbed is removed. Then, miners dig into the ground to extract the diamonds. Sometimes, miners pan for diamonds in alluvial deposits in rivers by filling a pan with sand, rinsing it under water, and shaking it until the diamonds fall to the bottom of the pan. Another method miners use to pan for diamonds is a **sluice**, which forces water through a sieve, separating the diamonds from the sand.

A miner pans for diamonds in a river in Kalimantan, Borneo, Indonesia.

Ocean deposits

Some diamonds are carried by rivers to the ocean. In the ocean, diamonds are mined by moving sand on the seabed to reveal the diamonds that have settled on the rock below. Suction pipes suck gravel and diamonds from the ocean floor to ships. The diamonds are separated from the gravel on board the ships and sent for processing.

Ships at sea extract ocean diamonds using remote-controlled underwater machines to remove the top layer of ocean floor, and then dig up the diamond-bearing sand.

World Diamond Deposits

Today, diamonds are mined in many parts of the world. Most of the more valuable diamonds come from Botswana in southern Africa. Russian diamonds are mostly found in northern Siberia. Diamonds are also mined in China, Guyana, India, Venezuela, and Canada.

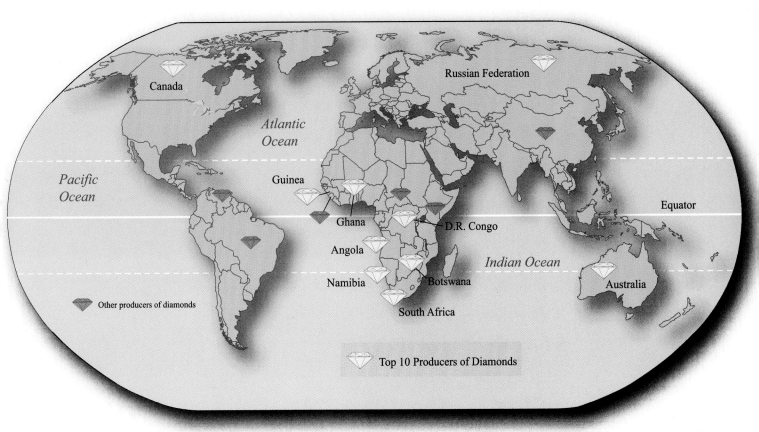

(left) A ruby mine in Burma.

Underground mines

Once digging has begun at open-pit mines, the underground deposits can be reached. Shafts are sunk down to horizontal drifts, or passageways, into the pipe. The kimberlite rock is drilled and blasted, so the rocks above the tunnel cave in. The broken rock is then scraped out of the tunnel in a bucket attached to a cable, loaded into cars, and moved to an underground crusher.

Mining kimberlite pipes

Prospectors searching for diamonds look for the distinctive bluish stone of a kimberlite pipe. When they find it, they make a map to plan the mine. First they excavate, or dig, a pit into the pipe. This type of mine is called open-pit, or open-cast, and is dug in steps, or benches. Next, miners drill and blast the hard rock, then remove the broken material.

A kimberlite mine

blue ground

mining tunnel

Environmental concerns

Like all mines, diamond mines pose a threat to the natural environment. Diamond mining companies spend millions of dollars a year to prevent, and clean up environmental damage. Mining companies use buried pipelines to control soil **erosion** surrounding mines, and **non-toxic** chemicals reduce risk from pollutants.

Diamonds were discovered in Canada's Northwest Territories in 1991. Today, Canada is the world's third largest diamond producer.

Smuggle proofing

Diamond mining companies have always been concerned about theft in their mines. In the 1900s, mines in South Africa began to take their concerns so seriously that they performed physical exams on miners leaving mines after their work day was done. The physical exams led to even more degrading treatment and procedures for miners. In the 1990s, the De Beers company developed an x-ray machine to see inside the bodies of miners and ensure that they did not swallow any of the company's diamonds, in order to sell them later for their own profit.

A doctor looking for stolen diamonds examines a miner.

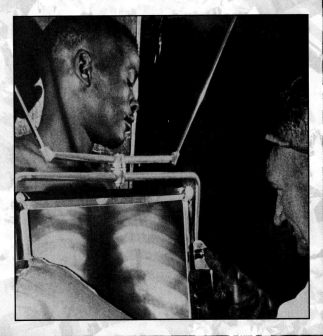

Processing Gems

After they are mined, diamonds and other gemstones are processesed before they are sold. They are graded, cut, and polished. Once a gemstone has been cut and polished, it is called a gem.

Up to Grade

Just 50 percent of all diamonds mined in the world are gem quality. The rest are used in industry as abrasives, or for use on hard tipped drills. After diamonds are mined, they are separated into categories: gem-quality, near gem-quality, and industrial-grade. Diamonds are graded into stones of similar type or size, such as "over one karat but less than fifteen karats." The term smalls refers to diamonds between one karat and 1/10 karat, while Sands, are less than 1/10 karat. Stones are also sorted by shape. Only a diamond can cut a diamond, so diamonds of lesser value are used to shape diamonds of greater value.

The brilliant cut is the most popular cut for diamonds.

In the cut

Diamonds can reflect light, bend it, or break it into all the colors of the rainbow. To achieve the greatest **brilliance**, diamond cutters, or specially trained people called lapidaries, cut tiny sides, or facets into the stone. For the diamond to have the greatest sparkle, the size, shape and angle of these facets must be exactly right.

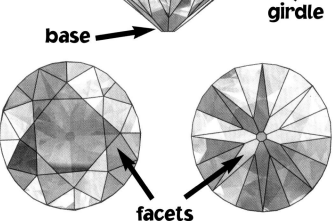

table

girdle

base

facets

Multi-faceted

All diamonds have a grain that makes for a better cut, cleave, or slice. When the cut is against the grain, the diamond is sawed. This is done by a thin disk, coated with a mixture of olive oil and diamond dust. The disk revolves at 5,000 times a minute. The diamond is bruted, or cemented in a lathe, then ground against another diamond. The final step in diamond cutting is the grinding and polishing of the facets to a high brilliance.

Finished stone

Cut diamonds are sent to sorters who separate them based on shape, color, size, and clarity. The stones go to factories to be polished into finished gems. The main centers for diamond cutting are in Antwerp, Belgium, New York, U.S.A., Tel Aviv, Israel, and Bombay, India.

(above) A rough diamond is examined through a magnifying loop.

(left) A diamond is polished using a machine that grinds nicks from the diamond's surface.

(below) Popular gem shapes are oval-shaped, rose-cut, cabochon, pear, marquise, and emerald.

     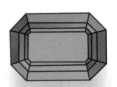

21

Rough to refined

When diamonds or gemstones are mined, they do not look like the gleaming gems in jewelers' windows. They look like irregular shaped, dull pebbles. The change from rough stone to dazzling gem, involves the skills of a lapidary.

(above) A diamond polisher looks at the diamond through a lupe before polishing.

(above) A diamond cutter does precision work in a finishing shop in Johannesburg, South Africa's Jewel City.

Neat and precise

Learning to be a lapidary, requires years of training and painstaking work. Diamond and gem cutters need strong eyesight, hand and finger **dexterity,** and good eye-hand coordination. Diamond workers must be neat and precise and have strong powers of concentration. Most lapidaries apprentice, or learn, from experienced cutters. It takes about three years to become a lapidary.

A bloody history

Many of the world's diamond deposits are located in countries that are poor, at war with other countries, or involved in civil wars. For many years, the world's largest diamond producer, South Africa, was an apartheid state. Under apartheid, black South Africans were forced to live seperately from white South Africans. Most of the laborers in the diamond mines were black men who were separated from their families for months or years and paid little for their work. Apartheid ended in South Africa in 1992, and conditions in diamond mines improved. In other areas of Africa, wars still rage in diamond rich areas. The diamonds mined and sold to fund the wars are called conflict, or blood, diamonds. The **United Nations** has called on buyers not to purchase conflict diamonds. By asking for a "certificate of origin" for rough or uncut diamonds, buyers can ensure their diamonds are not funding bloody civil wars.

Miners dig a gravel pit at a conflict diamond mine in the Democratic Republic of Congo. The African country has suffered through many years of war and terror, funded partly through diamond sales.

Gems at Work

The most widespread use of diamonds and gemstones is decorative, but the hardness of diamonds, rubies, and sapphires also makes them valuable for use in industry.

Diamonds in industry

Diamonds that have flaws or are of poor color are used in industry. Manufacturers can set whole diamonds into tools or bake crushed diamonds into cutting tools. These tools are used to cut and shape the hard metals used to make automobiles, airplanes, and other machinery. Wheels made of crushed diamonds sharpen other tools and grind glass lenses. Diamonds are also used in saws and drill bits, clocks, and lasers.

Diamonds are set into drill bits that miners use to bore through rock.

Diamonds in medicine

The very hard surface of diamonds makes them useful for making surgical scalpels, or knives. Doctors use them because they are many times sharper than regular steel blades. Incisions, or cuts, made with diamond-edged scalpels heal faster than those made with a steel blade. Diamond scalpels are used in sensitive types of surgery, such as removing cataracts, or the cloudy covering over the lenses of people's eyes.

Diamonds are used in electronics as wire drawing dies, which means that wires can be pulled through tiny holes in the diamonds to keep the wires in place.

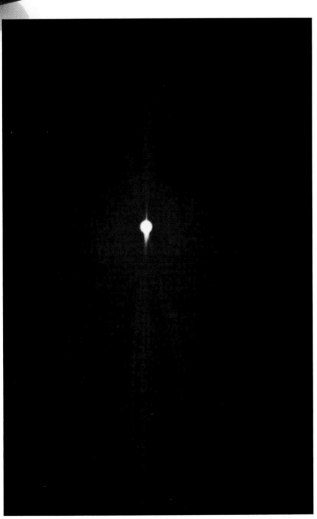

Gemstones in time

Today, most watches use quartz crystals to run, but in the past watches had fifteen or more tiny rubies and sapphires inside their mechanisms. A watch's mechanism is the parts that make it run, such as the **gears**. Rubies and sapphires were used to keep the bridges that join the sets of gears in place, so that the watch kept perfect time. The hardness of the gems prevented wear and tear to the mechanism.

Rubies made by humans, called synthetic rubies, are used in lasers. Ruby lasers create a powerful beam of red light.

Synthetic diamonds and gemstones

Diamonds and other gemstones are very rare and expensive to mine. For many years, scientists have tried to use modern technology to create gemstones in a laboratory. In 1902, scientists were successful in making rubies, sapphires, and other gemstones using a substitute for corundum called aluminum oxide. Gemstones that are made by scientists are called synthetic gemstones. In 1954, the first synthetic diamond was made by compressing carbon under extremely high heat and pressure. Today, several companies produce synthetic diamonds, most of which are used in industry.

Synthetic diamonds are almost identical to real diamonds, but they are made in laboratories by scientists and used mainly for industrial purposes.

Cubic zirconia looks so similar to a real diamond, jewelers use special tests to tell them apart.

Imitation diamonds

Synthetic diamonds are made from carbon, the same element as diamonds, but many other substances can look like diamonds from the outside. These substances are called imitation diamonds. Some imitation diamonds are natural, such as the colorless version of the gemstone zircon. Zircon sparkles like a real diamond but is softer and will scratch more easily. The **artificial** substance cubic zirconia is used to make cheap imitation diamonds for jewelry.

Lore and Legend

Diamonds and gemstones have intrigued people for centuries and many stories have grown around their beauty and mystery. Some of these stories are true, while others are myths that have changed over time.

The emperor's crown

The Crown of the Andes, a magnificent jeweled crown, is said to have belonged to Atahualpa, the last emperor of the Inca peoples of Peru. It contained 453 emeralds totalling 1523 karats. When the Spanish **conquered** Peru and captured the king in 1,532, they stole the crown. It went missing and reappeared in the United States in the 1940s, without its emeralds. They were stolen and set in jewelry that was sold to wealthy people.

The disappearance of the legendary emeralds from The Crown of the Andes is shrouded in mystery.

The Valley of the Diamonds

According to a Greek myth, all the diamonds in the world came from a deep valley in what is now northern India. Giant serpents guarding this valley would kill anyone who looked at them. The famous explorer-conqueror Alexander the Great (355 B.C.-323 B.C.) is said to be the only person to ever reach this mystical spot. To conquer the snakes, Alexander placed a giant iron mirror where they lived, so they would see themselves and die. Even with the serpents gone, no one would go into the valley to collect the gems. Alexander asked his advisors what to do and he was told to throw a piece of flesh into the valley. The diamonds stuck to the flesh, and the birds snatched it in their beaks and flew away. Alexander's people followed the birds and caught the diamonds as they fell from the meat and dropped to the ground.

Arm-sized ruby

The Italian explorer Marco Polo traveled to Asia in the 1200s and brought back a story of an enormous ruby. The King of **Ceylon** owned the gem, said to be nine inches (23 centimeters) long and thick as an arm. When Kublai Khan, the Emperor of China offered an entire city in exchange for the amazing gem, the king turned him down, refusing to part with his ruby at any price.

Find your birthstone

Birthstones have been popular good luck symbols since ancient times. Each month is assigned a gemstone. The gemstones are said to have special qualities that reflect the personalities of people born in the month and what the stone represents, such as good health, loyalty, friendship, and happiness.

January - garnet
Stands for loyalty and friendship and brings the owner good health.

February - amethyst
Brings peace of mind and drives worries away.

March - aquamarine
Protects health and is good for people who love the sea.

April - diamond
Strengthens body and soul, protects innocence and brings out a person's best qualities.

May - emerald

Emeralds bring joy, and help tell the future, and sharpen the mind.

June - pearl

A pearl is understated but precious, like the person who wears it.

July - ruby

Gives people born in July vigor, good fortune, and love.

August - peridot

Brings friendship, helps ward off envy, depression and fear.

September - sapphire

Relaxes and clears the mind and protects from fraud, envy, and ill health.

October - opal

Ensures fidelity and confidence; sharpens the mind and, according to legend, is good for the eyes.

November - citrine

Brings lightheartedness, relaxes the body and helps clean it of toxins.

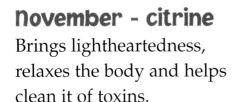

December - blue topaz

Is a symbol of fidelity and love and gives the wearer patience and a pleasant attitude.

Glossary

alluvial Soil and debris moved by water and wind found in rivers, streams, and dry streambeds

artificial Made by human craft

atom The smallest unit of an element

brilliance The amount of light a gemstone reflects

carbon An element found in all living things

Ceylon An island below India, now called Sri Lanka

chemical A substance produced by chemistry

conquer To aquire and rule by force

dexterity Skill and ease in using the hands

durable Long lasting

element A substance that cannot be broken down into smaller parts by chemical means

erosion To wear away over time

extinct No longer existing in living or active form

fossilize To preserve in a substance, such as rock or amber, over time

gear A wheel with teeth that fits into another wheel, causing both to turn

karat The unit of measurement used to weigh diamonds equal to 0.007 ounces (200 milligrams)

Latin The language of the ancient Romans

magma Hot melted rock formed within the Earth

mantle The area between the Earth's core and crust

mineral A natural, non-living substance made up of one or more elements

monopoly Complete control over a product or industry

non-toxic Not poisonous

organic Something that was once alive

organism An individual live plant or animal

pressure Continuous force against an object by another object touching it

prospector A person who searches for diamonds, gemstones, or other valuable minerals

radiography Photography that uses radiation other than natural light, such as X-rays

refract To deflect or bend light

sluice A sieve that sifts river water and separates diamonds from debris

supernatural Relating to existence outside of the natural world

United Nations An international organization that seeks to improve the lives of people around the world

Index

1 2 3 4 5 6 7 8 9 0   Printed in the USA   0 9 8 7 6 5 4 3 2 1